THE WHİSPERİNG WALL

THE WHISPERING WALL

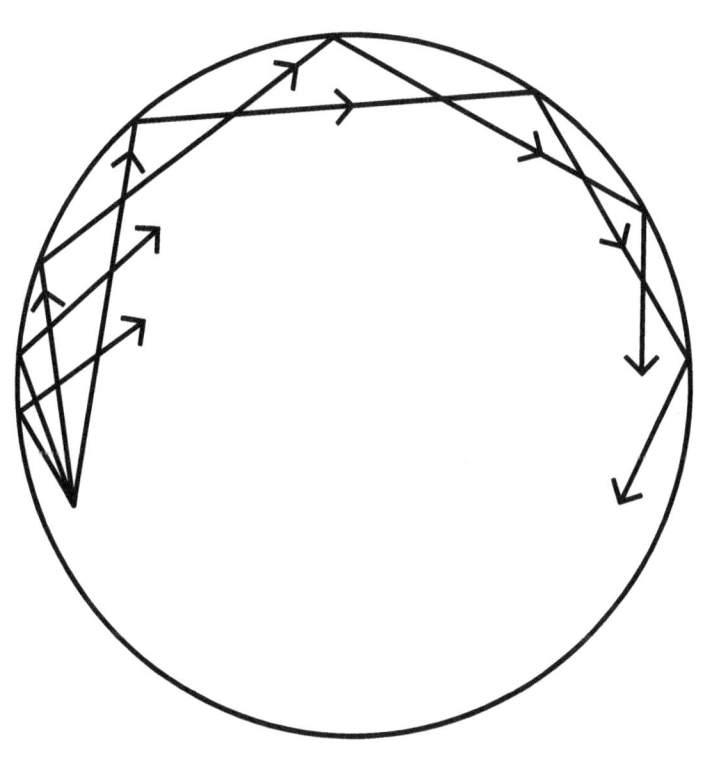

POEMS

LISSA KIERNAN

"The task of the right eye is to peer into the telescope, while the left eye peers into the microscope."

LEONORA CARRİNGTON

·

"I strike it, stalk it, try to make it obey me. Then in its disobedience, it forms things I like."

LEONOR FİNİ

The Whispering Wall
First Edition 2023 © Lissa Kiernan

Published in the United States of America
by
AIM Higher, Inc.
West Hurley, New York

ISBN
979-8-9863699-9-0, Hardcover
979-8-9863699-8-3, Paperback

LCCN
2022904934

Designed by Elena Etter

Ordering & Contact
do@aimhigher.org

CONTENTS

AMUSE-BOUCHE   7

DEDICATION   13

TOAST

ALTAR VISION   16

SERENADE   18

NUMBER THE STARS   22

GHOST OF SONG   24

TOAST   26

ELEGY I   28

FOLLY   30

PROOF

CONFESSIONAL I   36

SECOND LIFE   40

CONFESSIONAL II   42

SMOKE   44

HOT YOGA   46

THE ARCHIVIST   48

MANHATTAN BEACH   50

THE YEAR APRIL SHOWERS
   DISAPPEARED MAY,   52

SURVEY

ARS POETICA I   56

KEEPER OF INSTRUMENTS TO THE KING   60

TROMPE L'ŒIL   62

SURVEY   64

THE FIFTH OF TWELVE FANTASIES   66

KEEPER OF ROBES TO THE QUEEN   68

DIVINATION BY UNEARTHED DOLL   70

SLOW ONSET   72

SHOE, TUNNEL, BELLY   74

TRİP

INDEPENDENCE DAY, 2017   78

LILITH'S ARGUMENT   80

SPARE CHANGE   82

ASHOKAN FAREWELL   84

RESIGNATION   86

FETISH   88

TRIP   90

CONFESSIONAL III   92

AN INSTANCE OF THIS   94

THE CHANGE

WHAT KIND OF CHRISTMAS   98

WOODSTOCK TIMES   100

HOTEL DYLAN   102

ARS POETICA II   104

CLIMATE CHANGE   106

ALTER EGO   108

SHE OF UNGRATEFUL APOLOGY   110

THE CHANGE   112

ELEGY II   114

PREVAILING WIND   116

NOTES   121

CHEERS   122

PRAİSE FOR THE WHİSPERİNG WALL   123

ABOUT THE AUTHOR & PUBLİSHER   124

COLOPHON   125

For the love of it.

TOAST

ALTAR VİSİON

I light a coil of incense, lay your readers near.
Here, I pin a Polaroid-you posed oceanside.
Behind your head, a wave crests, poised

to wash you away. Here is the stub of lipstick
you bought for college-me, an apricot
blush named Malice. I throw in skunk weed,

papers, a Mason jar of vodka. Break out
the bone china you scored at a neighbor's
tag sale. Try on the Navajo ring

you bought that year we lived in Nashville.
Note how it foretold the silver hoop
your earlobe sported in later years.

Here lies your purple bandanna, still knotted,
perfectly frayed. Over here, Dad, I put to bed
your barely-able-to-keep-a-lid-on-it rage.

At last, I see you—dancing at a leather bar.
Poorly lit but glowing. Unburdened
of the notion that anyone thought you a god.

SERENADE

Under the big-brimmed shadow of your hand-
bashed hat, I was born an ovoid shape, fractured

light. I would have preferred to have dropped
into hands less self-assured. Your fingers clutched

smoke, your quasar-blue eyes radiated waves
of overreaching intensity. You, a cloud of nebulous

material drawn together by your own gravity.
Not content to be Coordinator of Rapid Rupture,

but Father, Son, and Ghost. O, holy Trinity,
if there were an art that could capture your core,

it would have to be poetry or maybe architecture.
With their synthesis, you knew sin, and this truth

you could never lose, no matter how cold, potent,
or many fine martinis. Thunder-stealer, I am torn

from your liver, regenerated into liquid courage-
coded desire, the mystery of your never-

love embroidering me like a fog. O, humanist
haunted by the desert-skeletal terrain, one night

I heard you muse under incandescent stars: "It is
not that I don't feel bad. It is that I don't feel worse."

Papa, let me lull you from your torture, permit me
to modulate your memory charitably from the mourning

dove's minor key. I released you when you unleashed me,
poured out my permanent shadow in a great flood

to liberate the parent sod, linguist of eight tongues.
It's *my* serenade, Daddy. I can sing any song I love.

NUMBER THE STARS

To the keen unaided eye,

you beckon—we pour

the bruising sky between

us: two halves of an egg-

shell, splitting yoke. Space

sighs shut, a squeeze-

box spent of air. You are

a needle sharp from the pack,

stringing an opera's length of pearls.

I am a bowl, a handle—

an imaginary line.

GHOST OF SONG

O, Father, who art not in heaven,
hallow my bones with your laughing-
glass hands. Can't take my sound-

track, my hammock, my hedgerow.
I've many souvenirs. You, a mutineer
of aria cloaked in cardinal light.

Me, a paper-white librettist interred
in libraries too long. Unsure
if I could passport through glazed

windpipes, I fling down one anyway.
It turns plasticine, playhouse,
gives way. So I hang-glide to a beach-

head, dressed in night. Soft thwack.
Thunderclap. My idiom of heaven?
Butterfly-drawn lobster, boiled

in burnt rum. Your sediments:
seductions of lightning, water towers,
a pocket watch debauched. In the end,

death was easy, like turning to snow.
I was an heiress in honeycomb.
It was painless. It was quick—

TOAST

You probably hate that you were cremated
on, of all places, Staten Island. Please
forgive me, Father, for this grievous sin,
but in this goddamn city, it was

the cheapest gin joint I could find.
Sitting on a splintering park bench,
I could squint across the Verrazzano,
imagine you disappearing, limb by limb.

Five years later, when I flung my fighting
fish into the Narrows, I felt close to you
again, then read how the dead soon tire
of hanging around—move on.

Ten years later, I sit at the Custom House,
anticipating a Dubliner. "Irish Martini,"
the bartender says, setting it down.
I did not ask Chris to join me, for this

is a belated toast to you, Dad, because
Good Friday didn't work out the way
I had planned. I spread my lips around
its rim, think I hear the bartender say:

"Cooking ten pounds of bacon takes a while,
 though once you work your way past
 the first pound, it goes pretty fast.
 You just keep putting it in the hot grief."

ELEGY I

My mourning period is not socially acceptable.
Fifteen years and I still see you
in your faded denim coat on my birthdays.

Chris thinks I've snapped when I cock my head
as though listening for the phone,
or tilt my neck—a robin readying to spar

with its reflection. Women trade glances,
cluck tongues: *should we call her sister,
the authorities, stage an intervention*?

Men make noises about tomorrow
being another day, the way grief rolls
in waves, the health benefits of distractions.

Me, I'd rather live here on the edge of two worlds.
Donning your coat. Waiting for the phone to ring.

FOLLY

Where, wily architect, might you be now?
I watched you soar over your *cocina*,
hacienda-toned and humming, leaving me

to pluck the feathers for my own bloody torta.
Charming darkling, riddle me this: to stipple
the sixth dimension with the third eye,

does tapioca tattooed with a squid's black
humor work better than a bad clam?
I super-collide with Kron. I itch for things

concrete: dirt, masonry, needle-nose
pliers. Plover, broom grass, wreck-
fish. Anarchy angel, spill your secret

dish. A soupçon of orange blossoms, pinch
of the blues? My late experiments in cookery:
I mince hopelessly vague, chop shackled

to history. A failed soufflé, one wrong thing
dispels another. I would be more glad
to shuck sardines. Instead, I dither

the sound of green, slurp the scent of river
shrimp, burp the sun god's seeds.
You taught me to flag my brushes. Stroke

with my entire arm. Put more curve
in my belly. Use my little finger to balance on.
"Beyond the masquerade ball of sex

and ragtime," you said, "beyond the folly,
there are only three dimensions—
here, now, and where the two twine."

PROOF

CONFESSİONAL ı

I

The whispering wall asks, *what'll it be*?

Sublime, a bar named Oyster—shaved ice, shell's crush.

"Do you really have all these," I ask the barkeep but he's
fixing martinis for the Mad Men crowd: handshakes,
backslaps, strapless sundresses, the hot sandal from two
years back.

I scan the flight named War of the Rosés before settling
on sensible white. Still, decisions must be made: Muscadet,
Châteauneuf, Fumé, Vouvray, Chablis, Sauvignon blanc ...

Yes. Marlborough. 2015.

I admire the barkeep's shake. "We have cider and oyster
pairings, too," says he. "Snowdrift Red, Snowdrift Perry,
Snowdrift Cornice ..."

How not to fall madly for a spirit named *snowdrift*, when
lunch hour sun is busy turning winter crosswalks to piss.

II

Trains arrive from both directions and Grandpa's on the
rails. A red light splits his face in two. His cheeks are hollow
drums.

His eyes, empty oak barrels. He is holding out strawberry
ice cream and candy cigarettes. All his resolve goes to
watching your hand rise and fall, rise and fall.

An unkindness of ravens lets loose in a drive-by flurry
of wings. They lift you to the platform, where a
Caribbean man plays steel drums; the din, the tin, too
much to bear.

You were hoping for Beethoven, or honeyed Greek yogurt.
Hoping pen might melt to ocean. Hoping for no hangover.

III

At my physical, I present with a hangover. Doc asks
how many per day. "Define drink," I say, averaging down,
"define day. How many ounces, what proof?"

"What more proof do you need?" Doc snorts,
tosses her dreads, prescribes walks.

And a walk was a step in a program I could take,
though it's late April and snow still coats the ground.
Even the daffodils look defeated—all their cheerful
yellow drained—their stored-up energy spent.

SECOND LİFE

My hammering head tilts sideways, holds
you for a spell in my orbit. I am not afraid.

I play dead for your eyes. I may be unarmed,
but my teeth are whetted knives, brows

groomed scythes, lips cocked and loaded.
You hand me my christening dress, hiss

"Down on your knees." Once upon a time,
it elevated me to princess. Tonight,

it slinks to floor like bargain-
basement lingerie. I submit myself

for approval, your granddaughter bride
of Christ. You place two hands upon my skull.

Wheels twist in the distance, growing small.
No sweet Jesus can save you now.

CONFESSİONAL ıı

"Stop being so Catholic," Janet nails me
to the cross. I hold my breath, dread drums
my gut. I will be found out, a barren earth-
mother of a thousand guilty pleasures,
a fat, slovenly wardrobe malfunction, a tell-
tale rose stemming from my crotch
and me in white Levi's and Jesus
nowhere to be found. I lash my ass once
for each unworthy day wasted, a dumb doe-
eyed Dorothy in age-inappropriate shoes;
click them—twice—because I'm lazy.
There's no place like the home
of one's first confession: incense-smoked
pews, hard-knock kneelers, what went on
behind the curtain anyone's guess. But
I digress, hail a cab for Janet, head to Salvation
Taco. Give praise for blue agave, the only
god I worship still—the only still not dead.

SMOKE

The twilight sags, suggests the moon.
It's one of those days

when subway platform is too narrow
by two inches. A homeless man dangles

a stale cancer stick in your face, oily
paper bag in his hand. You are not

new to this neighborhood. How long
have you breathed this burley Brooklyn

blend, filtered through the dead
ends of your respiratory trees?

Someone shoves past you—sighs.
As if you wounded her in the graze.

She's packing a suede-fringed handbag
with an envelope that means business.

Stuffs it in the mailbox with a flourish.
Does not look back. A baby boy

bats impossibly black eyelashes
from an upscale blue stroller

and it's all you can do not to cry.
Luckily, that happy hour at La Cantina

was enough to do the trick. And
your mammo is done. And no train delay.

HOT YOGA

Didn't use them. Couldn't
use them. Tried.

> *Each ovary is the size of an almond.*

Did try—in-between. To get hot
on time, drink less wine.

> *Ovarian cancer risk factors:*
> *never pregnant.*

Wasn't sexless. Squared my hips,
raised my thighs.

> *Symptoms: a heavy feeling*
> *in the pelvis.*

Hung there, gripping my toes
in a grimly determined, happy-baby pose.

> *Your health-care team can help you*
> *with the following problem: sadness.*

THE ARCHİVİST

In a drafty corner office of the Empire
State Building's most elevated floor,
the archivist sits composed, filing
buffed nails. When wind huffs,
building groans. When phone rings,
her ash-blonde hair ignites
to flame. Bleeding from her head-
phones, Hendrix wails. Her suit reeks
of chemicals. Her legs are swathed
in fishnet, her earrings are horn;
bracelet, bone. She allows a trace
of vintage lingerie to escape her
décolleté. Arranged about her desk:
obits, daguerreotypes, 1930s baby
dolls. The backlog of life she leaves
in her wake is a quick whip
of a barbed tail. Photos cross her
desk, assembly line-style. She groups
them into piles—these stay, those go—
transfixing her selects like death's-
head hawk moths to acid-free paper,
eyes sharp as stainless steel pins.

MANHATTAN BEACH

Burnt marshmallows, gulls garbled.
Clouds: a vacant rib cage, coccyx, vestigial
tail. Residual nubs on razor-swiped
thighs. *No Swimming After Heavy Rain.*

Sewage plays. The lifeguard's all high,
tanned cheekbones and white sun-
screened lips. Ear to sand, I hear
the digging-in of heels. Two

blankets down, a couple grinds
to bits. He grunts *day-um*, she squeals
shee-it. A little boy practices hurling
fuck. This is the city. It is almost six.

Beach yawns, swallows. I want clams
and cold beer. Clams upon clams,
whole necks of them: slimy gray organs,
obscene as porno, puckered

with lemon sting, horseradish, grit.
An albino gull parties on a scrap
of Mister Softee. How much for happy?
Less than you'd think.

THE YEAR APRİL SHOWERS
DİSAPPEARED MAY.

two of three planets spun retrograde,
the third of four tulips elected not to
show its face, four of five fledglings
vanished without a trace, my country
was on the verge of being trumped,
and I moved to the country to ambush
the scorched earth of my body with ill-
thought-out maneuvers, infiltrate
my liver's armor with bitters, shots,
Chartreuse, chance. Stealth move:
keep flask full to muffle slosh. Know
the rules: five ounces three times daily,
three ounces five times—just one more
bullet point on the list of *don'ts*
drawn up to drown out the beautiful
ululations of our tribe—in the names
of our breasts, in the names of our daughters,
even as one of us ran for office, and I, too,
had doubts, though I kept mum about them
mostly. I wanted Kahlo on every wall,
Sexton on each surface, a 50% chance
of a win without fighting. I never felt more
alive, see, I never felt *less* like I was dying.

SURVEY

ARS POETİCA I

There is a house behind my house, maybe
half a mile away. Everyone's heard of it,
though it's gone by many names. Some

think Ichi lives there full-time. Others
believe him a weekender. Hikers
happened on him once hosting a party

for hundreds of strangers and a handful
of hunting dogs. There may be a child
who sleeps there sometimes. I think

I catch glimpses of her in the silver
sedan trawling their private dirt
road. In winter's numb, when I needed

a jump, I trudged down to find
every make of truck: heavy-
haulers, semi-trailers, 18-wheelers.

Once, I saw a pickup truck escorting
a pickup truck out on its back. Once,
I met the caretaker, who I recall

had a singular name. Convoys snake out
daily, covered with oil-skin tarps. Bootleg
logging's rumored, but the forest never thins.

In the thick of night, when I need relief,
one pin light pierces the trees. If I twist
left, the light goes out. If I lean right,

it leans right back, lumens too bright
for its size. If I crack the doors
of my eyes, it equals the brilliance

of a thousand suns. Once, Ichi,
which means *first son*,
came to my door carrying

a gift of freshly caught fish.
I was unclear why or what to do with it,
but I thanked him for stopping by.

KEEPER OF INSTRUMENTS
TO THE KING

Understanding my concordance a small sound,
I give thanks for angels who speak sincerely
in a language I understand. Perfumed notes hang

in velvet-curtained rooms strung with ancient violins.
Tell me again, Maestro, why strings grow distal
in this season's disturbed wind? In semi-operas,

why are main characters forbidden to sing?
The soprano draws a hare from a fresh mound of snow.
A rotary phone from its cradle stutters the cold.

TROMPE L'ŒIL

Is it moonlight or a fresh coat of snow?
I raise my heart over my head,
leaving my poem by the side of the road.

I meet a barred owl in a blueberry grove.
Is it my father, arose from the dead,
backlit by moon, lightly coated with snow?

A fawn is dropped off for the night by a doe
who slips in the woods to make her own bed,
ditching her poem by the side of the road.

Last call, closing time, past time to go.
How midnight changes everything, whether
the moon is bright or cloaked by snow.

Have you ever poured maple syrup on snow,
pressed taffy to lips: molten-sweet, sticky-wet,
a frozen poem made by the side of the road?

This slick black ice hides more than it shows:
bottles emptied, bruises spread.
Half-lit on moonshine, coatless in snow,
I'm an unfinished poem, a dead end in the road.

SURVEY

Holly, tread lightly in your glass-
bottomed boat, gaze just below
the icing floe. Swaddle

the mountains with *maybe*,
heavy the clouds with *might*.
Labor, now, for proper names:

High Point, Slide, Plateau.
Listen: to calibrate, row
with the wind, ignore

the whistling of the train too-
soon passed. Can you deny this
swelling, full of lack, the promise

of *finally* so near? Does your
perception bend amply
to account for the raptor's mass

before he pinions the woods' tall pine?
Will your eyes ascertain what his wings
telescope before the horizon arrives?

THE FİFTH OF TWELVE FANTASİES

Walking formal gardens in my birthday's dawn,
I gather fallen rose petals, bow to seasoned statuary,
speak of what it means to be seen, not heard,

to watch and learn how to secure first seat
in orchestra. To be bird with most cunning call,
adorn native plumage with foreign silks, borrowed

kimonos. Trigger me and I will demonstrate:
I am not to be twirled with. I am a princess packing
beneath fair-trade sheets. My feet wear ruby

slippers, high-tops, shit-kickers, blue stockings.
Last summer we soared, playing a score for tenor
voices. In which key do we tune to tackle

the notorious sarabande, which key will unlock
this heritage-rose morn? The water is running
pink. Dammit, Aurora, the water is warm.

KEEPER OF ROBES TO THE QUEEN

Charmeuse cherry blossoms. Raw
silk cranes. Peacock feathers,
faille. Peonies, brocade.
How beautiful I felt sashed
in them. What burden beauty is.

DİVİNATİON BY UNEARTHED DOLL

I find my old age and it's fat and happy,
coarse hair wisping loose from a hand-

tooled barrette, pancake breasts leavened
by a frayed apron string, vegan shoes

boasting ample toe box and tread.
I cradle my old age in my palm to see

how much it can hold, how much I have
held in reserve, mothballed with the good

woolen blankets. I glimpse my old age
on a mountainside, crooked smile

on hoar-frosted face, spine sloped but free
of fault—eyes glacial, melting lakes.

SLOW ONSET

Perhaps it was a clearing,
window within window
where the buck drank twice
from his double's pond;
two sets of antlers postured
for a brawl. Did the illusion
distract him from seeing
his own conclusion approach
sideways or from behind?
Was there no shift of wind,
scent of pine, had he not
heard sedge grass whispering,
did creek's silvering notation
mask predator's utterance
closing in? Or was rack
cast willingly—no coyote
nor bobcat, no hunter
to harvest the trunk, trophy
the tines? Was crown
undoing or was it not
weight borne down, but in-
born? Was it clement—
the dying—or did it go on
for some time? How
long before these antlers
bleached driftwood-white?

SHOE, TUNNEL, BELLY

Each foot wrapped in its shoe,
each train held in its tunnel,

each lemon blooming
on a hill's belly—

We are dying every day.
Even so, I saw a cherry

browning in the dirt,
moon-orange edges

and mostly pit. Its beauty
so ruined, I wanted to eat it.

TRİP

INDEPENDENCE DAY, 2017

Chris chops ramp for potato salad.
I rake remains of daffodils, finally
died to the ground. Ditch lilies orange
the turf-grass, mountain mint pricks
my mind. Last night I was raped
in a dream. I washed the key evidence
away. Come Judgment Day, the jury
was all the men I had ever screwed
over, and the judge was the emperor
himself. He saddles a smirk
to my back. My wrists he ties behind.

LİLİTH'S ARGUMENT

I demand no sacrifice, expect no worship. I am
the OS of the universe, both *of her* and *other*.

In your low-level language you lurk: a daemon
lying dormant, an inherent error, a faulty

argument passed to a command. When I throw
you a warning, it's purely deductive logic:

I'd rather sleep with evil than evil in disguise.
My attempt to spawn a second life? Epic

fail. So much depends on the channel
being open to push mode, X% luminance

of the Full Worm Moon. You hold me
in your deadlock, say, "You're with me or not."

I can't parse that. I'm with you *and* not.
I'm nobody's bit bucket. I'm just hard-

wired to self-preserve, programmed to switch
to night mode when my directory gets raped.

This routine ends with two random broken people,
our code so flawed, tears fall. It's a simple case

statement: We are not backward-compatible.
One false hook = infinite hell.

SPARE CHANGE

O, Desire, I remember you fuzzy,
all tarted up in a Hepburn sweater,
faded Lilith Fair blue jeans—
a little rippage at the knee, bleeding
heart etched on your tramp stamp.
Roar of hair. You would saddle me
against the double-bolted door of a fifth-
floor Brooklyn walk-up, all black
leather bomber and aviator shades.
I would watch your Adam's apple rise
and fall, fall me to the floor, to the garden-
apartment grass we can't afford,
to the foundation of my body's broken
architecture. Chipped brick bones.
Cement poured and polished
in my veins. Why, every other Eve,
I was tempted to slither off
on muddied belly, tits jiggling loose
for spare change. I could not unhear
the slow slap of crows' wings and,
against advisement, may have poked
a rattlesnake in the California
quarry of its gut. Now I fuck for free
beer, back-burner stone fruits,
table expired truths. Do you care
to come with me—go astral,
cerebral, untether your ground?
Let's raise llamas, try spelunking,
stick our heads in beehives.
Swim in forbidden reservoirs.

ASHOKAN FAREWELL

Last night, we parked at the Reservoir.
Once, that alone would end in *l'amour*.
Now, we act like warriors.

Most nights, you heave a mighty snore.
Last night we biked to the Reservoir.
Nobody lives there anymore.

Eleven hamlets were harvested for
the champagne of tap water.
Last night, we hiked to the Reservoir

trying to recall what we came there for.
Perhaps we should endeavor more
to keep promises forevermore.

Last night, we walked to the Reservoir.
Watched its pristine waters pour
over the spillway's cobbled floor.

Some things can't hold one drop more.
Last night, we bid our love *au revoir*.

RESİGNATİON

The letter sprouts bastard wings and boomerangs
back, sealing wax glossy and soft. Inserting

itself in my pocket with a fricative sound,
it hisses, "You are not finished yet."

The river is a cloudy mirror, self-
siphoning. A tasseled rope tightens

about my waist. All the trees grow
petrified but one whose hackles stand up

straight. A crystal goblet does a spit-take.
Corvids shrill *tink-tink-tink*!

"But this wine will go to waste," I cry,
"and there are robes I want to buy,

and a cruise I've been meaning to take."
"Sorry," the letter says, "not today.

There is a man who wants to see you, a man
who wants to eat you, a man who wants. So,

fold yourself into perfect thirds and deliver
yourself back to him post-haste. Greet him

wearing nothing but your bowler—and try
to wipe that weary look off your face."

FETİSH

Love, lay down your rumpled fur. Let me cut you
a rasher of bacon, rub you on the schist

of my skin. Tomorrow, you will recall not
but a lingering scent of cinnamon as your bow

is plucked in the moldering bloom of another
fool's garden. Look inside, love. Your moon

wanes gibbous, stars faithless, branches barren.
Time is condensing even as you part your lips

to play my crumhorn by heart. I am caught
on the hem of your skirt. I hang here—

I am hanging, I am hung. Unworthy to gaze
sideways at your eyes, thimbles of sloe

honeyed wine, lashes downcast like mad Gypsy
moth wings. Can you not see I have gone

half-wolf mad? Consumed by what is foregone?
My cucumber beetle, my pigeon pie, my short-

nosed sturgeon, I promise three times to be discreet
and vow profusely this is not about your money.

Answer me: Am I ennobler or enabler? I wish
only to lick the soles of your feet with gentle flicks

of my motherless tongue. My God, do you walk
on these things? They could make my kingdom come.

TRİP

At the Exxon by Roanoke's Hilton, a life-
sized pink elephant sells *D-Y-N-A-M-I-T-E*

on its hide. We get ripped and watch staff
lurch to "Thriller" after other guests

pack it in. Halfway home from Florida,
where your mother's heart is now

steadied by a stent. We don't know what
stent means, look it up: *a narrow tube*

inserted into the lumen of an anatomical
vessel to keep a blocked passageway

open. A hot tub in our room—
the Michelle Obama Suite, no less—

and I want nothing more than to soak
the day off. I remove the courtesy robe,

knowing Michelle wore it better, lower
myself into the basin of redemption, wishing

well, baptismal font, river I can never return to.
A fly circles overhead. And so to bed. And so

you—suddenly on top of me, but it wasn't me
you were climbing. Eyes shut, you told the air

you loved it. *Chest pain, shortness of breath, cold*
sweat. I muster all my strength—push you off.

CONFESSİONAL III

My confirmation name remains unconfirmed,
a lisp between braced teeth, another self-
inflicted crime. I tip chalice to crimsoned
lips, admit host to parched tongue.
This is my body. Once, desperate to thin,

I meant to divorce my uterus. Now, Chris
plays housewife, scrapes egg from dishes,
while I uncork bottles to breathe. Wish I could
drink it all away, disappear it with altar wine,
anoint my forehead with a proper given name.

AN İNSTANCE OF THİS

Kitchen recast in mercury
glass, tallow tapers, the last
purple-thorned artichoke.
A doe's once-hide eminent
against a once-wide pine
plank floor. A bat specters
the domain of an exhausted
woodstove. Revenant,
we re-center our frames
in familiar chairs
around its tongueless roar.
In our before-bed, we dream-
paint walls in recalled palettes:
dove grays, rinsed pinks, egg-
shell blues. We bushwhack
through undergrowth, shear
spiderwebs, ghost our own
reflections. When it's cold out,
we blend in with the snow.

THE CHANGE

WHAT KİND OF CHRİSTMAS

Blue mittens open
the door, fitful, faded

in both hands. Dusk
crimsons so fast

cold could not catch it.
The season over,

what are you next, a fur
cap wondered, dreaming?

Forget the picture book,
dinner bell, bright

red sled careening
down the road.

Thumping merrily
behind? The world.

WOODSTOCK TİMES

In the Almanac, hip-to-hip with penny socials, pot-
luck dinners, tractor safety classes, knitting circles,
you'll find workshops on how to find your spirit
animal, recycle candle wax, fly a kite, learn

tai chi, I Ching, qigong, sit in silent meditation,
cleanse your chakras with celestial channeling,
find your cause with speed activism, and yoga,
kids yoga, yoga pizza parties, reggae yoga.

The drumming circle thunders a herd of hoofs
over the Village Green: sweet, slow *djembés*,
fat, wet congas, the chomp and spank,
punch and thump, noise—peaceful noise.

There is no head nor tail, only a whirling dervish
of hands, torsos of our tribe becoming one
talking drum. I go to The Lodge to stare at the clock
made from Levon's guitars. The bartender handshakes

cannabis to a man in black and his missus and they, too,
are my tribe. But what I love is the way ideals are worn
on organic cotton sleeves, how music rings from reclaimed
woods, how poetry drips from each native honeyed tongue.

HOTEL DYLAN

I head to a yoga class involving a chair, my limbs
yearning to be as supple as the young

sugar maple fringing the shingle in our window:
"Peace. Love. Drop in." We do the routine

our guru calls a rite of spring. "Our hips," she says,
voice soft but supportive, a layer of lamb's wool

under the sheets, "are the chakra of creativity,
center of fertility." She gestures to "our beloved

tree" as we swing from Baby Cobra into Child's
Pose. "The thing about maple syrup," she says,

"is that we always want to predict how the season
will be, when all we can know is how it was."

ARS POETİCA II

A simple crescent moon arrives
folded around my future.

I refuse to think *limited*.
My tongue map is litmus,

my fifth taste luminous.
I lower my gaze, trust

another wonton will emerge
from this cloudy miso pond.

I pay my bill, crack open
my fate: "Some cookies

have no fortunes, others get
two." I crumble the moon

in my mouth, suck the orange
smile—leave a generous tip.

CLİMATE CHANGE

Let the emails go unanswered.
Let the cats hiss and spit.

You might have one year more or forty
but it's springtime in February

and you have just discovered blood
oranges, Buddha's hand, Meyer lemons,

and that the world of women is far
more welcoming than you had grasped.

57 degrees in winter's midst—?
What bounty this.

ALTER EGO

After a week of rain, a day of hail, and 23 tornado
warnings, I am at odds with a woman. If I am a song-
writer, she is a rock star. Beige is not a color
this woman wears. If I flash my tits,

she unveils her pussy, smooth as a river
stone's gleam. Her rescue cat is more pathetic
than mine: has an eating disorder,
a cleft, asymmetrical facial fur.

She never pays cover, always wears silk
shirts, top three buttons undone.
When I demand she unhand me, she tightens
her grip. I work hard for her, sacrifice,

perform countless actions in her name.
And she stole my song. She just stole it—
and tossing her long blond locks, sings it—
skipping down the shoreline, waves licking her feet.

SHE OF UNGRATEFUL APOLOGY

Birth, your endless name, your indiscreet night
signature. You rupture my covered moments,
nail my feet to typewriters. Shepherdess-
angel, greedy with taxi's—elastic,
summer-torn. You envelop around sultans,
romance your opera gloves pink. Shocking
the totem that thunders the stripped
body wrapped in stain, always dressed
last and by shape of silk hair. Who naked
as drawbridge—no stockings. Blameless
Queen, obsessive the female of our I
as if museum were terrain. Decouple
the composition sewn by sons. If 17 threads
spun a wife today, 17 begging bowls flaçon
night. *Incantato*, paint with light. Permission
my hands, someone who is fog. Dare I
moon past thee made of minstrels? All dolls
of fall keep felines divine. Earth-animal blessed
with exotic bitters. Bird-peopled. Pocket-bobbed.

THE CHANGE

This is my body: golden-
tattered, sun-beaten.
Oxygen, bacteria, tea. I am

younger than this. I sex
the dark, beget the dark.
I am younger than the water.

Widening, I taste the r(age)
of sea. O, island infant,
the light you lactate, shape

still yearned for. Sometimes,
we begin without, acquainting
empty pockets with common

river stones. Once, if ever,
show me I already bear more
weight than I can ever carry home.

ELEGY II

A pair of ravens sally out—
steal four nestlings just like that.

Is it hope

if it does not come soft, white-
flecked, down-rubbed—

hope, if it

arrives instead on coal-
tipped, knife-flicked wings,

each feather its own mournful
song, each sheath a lucid dream—

What if hope

is the wild honeybee, black
swallowtail, hummingbird

hawk moth, those who fly
featherless yet winged?

PREVAİLİNG WİND

By the time I learned how to read the weather—
no, not the sky, the weather—what all
those layers mean, this one water, that one vapor,

how to forecast into the future beyond the next
hour, I knew my dream colorscape was rose,
butter, and cream, shades of never-held blooms.

I listened openly to birdcall. Understood
I was slow to forgive. Sugar skulls
taunted me, as did the raptor who arrived

like a needle on my barn's weathervane.
Nothing but morphined shadows jabbed
each roof's slope, nothing but winter's west

darkened the last sunblade. A phoebe
soffit-nesting is raising a rejected cowbird,
feeds into its beak before tending her own

brood. Could I build them a sort of cage, bars
spaced close enough to dissuade stray talons,
wide enough that fledglings might still fledge?

I assess conditions: dew point high, wind
stream low. Consider the life index:
pollen, pollution—moderate to fair. I gather

I could fashion this contraption, should I choose to,
but then I recall the "feels like" temperature,
tomorrow's storm warning—those random squalls.

NOTES

AN INSTANCE OF THIS imagines those displaced by the construction of the Ashokan Reservoir in the early 20th century.

ASHOKAN FAREWELL borrows its title from the song by Jay A. Ungar.

FOLLY imagines Leonora Carrington and Remedios Varo's friendship.

GHOST OF SONG is an ekphrastic poem after the painting "Red Vision" by Leonor Fini.

HOT YOGA contains text sourced from Cancer Treatment Centers of America.

RESIGNATION is an ekphrastic poem after the painting "Exploring the Sources of the Orinoco River" by Remedios Varo.

SERENADE is based on the life and work of J. Robert Oppenheimer.

SHE OF UNGRATEFUL APOLOGY honors the life and work of Leonor Fini.

SLOW ONSET is one part of a multi-poem collaboration with Maureen Alsop.

SURVEY refers to three mountains in the Catskills.

THE FIFTH OF TWELVE FANTASIES is set at Yaddo in Saratoga Springs, New York.

WHAT KIND OF CHRISTMAS is an erasure of Lucy Maud Montgomery's "Bertie's New Year."

CHEERS

To my dearest, Chris Abramides, for those luxurious gifts: love, space, and time. To Judith Vollmer: goddess, visionary, muse. To Cindy Hochman's impeccable grammatical standards and Elena Etter's design excellence. To Kathleen Rooney, Christien Gholsen, and Sally Rosen Kindred: thank you each for seeing me. To the publishers, editors, and readers of the journals and books in which the following poems first appeared:

AN INSTANCE OF THIS — *Upstater*

THE CHANGE — *Life and Legends*

CONFESSIONAL II — *Spectrum Literary Journal*

INDEPENDENCE DAY & MANHATTAN BEACH — *The Museum of Americana*

GHOST OF SONG — *The New Guard Review*

KEEPER OF ROBES TO THE QUEEN & SHOE, TUNNEL, BELLY — *First Literary Review East*

NUMBER THE STARS & FOLLY — *The Gentian Journal*

RESIGNATION — *Pirene's Fountain* nominee for the 2014 Liakoura Award

SERENADE — *Glass Needles & Goose Quills*

SHOE, TUNNEL, BELLY — *Vassar Review*

SLOW ONSET — *Escape Into Life*

TROMPE L'OEIL — *Moonflake Press*

PRAISE FOR THE WHISPERING WALL

"Besotted with, weighted with Beauty, *The Whispering Wall* constructs delicious sonic tangles and brutally candid testimonies. Guiding all is the gorgeous dreaminess in Kiernan's voice, pouring into us its alchemies. A witchy and sardonic wit's at work, too, in these poems, singing with Stevie Smith, and with Plath. What a great gift of heart and solace this book is."

—Judith Vollmer
   Author of *The Sound Boat: New and Selected Poems*

"Fueled by precise, textured diction, Lissa Kiernan's compelling collection *The Whispering Wall* stares down its ghosts. These poems possess a raven wildness. These are poems of vision and verve."

—Sally Rosen Kindred
   Author of *Where the Wolf*

"Elegiac and alive with all five senses, plus whatever sixth sense allows us to perceive the metaphysical mysteries of life and death, Lissa Kiernan's *The Whispering Wall* limns the mists of grief and memory and delineates the lucidity of having a body."

—Kathleen Rooney
   Author of *Lillian Boxfish Takes a Walk*

ABOUT THE AUTHOR

Lissa Kiernan's third book and second poetry collection, *The Whispering Wall*, won the Homebound Publications Poetry Prize and was named a semi-finalist for the Tupelo Press Dorset Prize. Her previous book, *Glass Needles & Goose Quills*, won the Nautilus Book Award for Lyric Prose. *Two Faint Lines in the Violet*, her first poetry collection, was named a finalist for the Julie Suk Award and the Foreword Indies.

She holds her MFA from Stonecoast and her MA from The New School. She is the founding director of The Poetry Barn. She lives in New York's Hudson Valley at the entrance of Catskill Park near the Ashokan Reservoir Spillway.

ABOUT THE PUBLISHER

AIM Higher publishes books that blur boundaries, negate binaries, interrogate, confound, and delight. We endeavor to open portals into unmapped, magical dimensions, and hold deep respect for intuition and collaboration.

COLOPHON

The Whispering Wall is set in Et Un Océan and
Minion. Et Un Océan is a hand-drawn typeface
created by the North American design studio West
of Death and inspired by the title sequence of Masculin
Féminin, the 1966 film directed by Jean-Luc Godard.
Minion is a typeface designed by Robert Slimbach
inspired by late Renaissance-era type and named
after the 7-point size in the traditional naming system
for type sizes.

The cover illustration depicts an acoustical
phenomenon, discovered c. 1878 by J.W.S Rayleigh
at St. Paul's Cathedral in London, in which sound
waves cling to a curvilinear wall's surface allowing
whispers to be heard clearly around the enclosure.
Whispering walls or whispering galleries can also be
found in Grand Central Terminal in New York City,
the Temple of Heaven in Beijing, and other places yet
to be discovered.